VISUALIZATION SKILLS FOR READING COMPREHENSION

SIX-MINUTE THINKING SKILLS

WORKBOOK

HAPPY FROG PRESS

ISBN 978-1-7752852-4-3

Happy Frog Press

www.HappyFrogPress.com

INTRODUCTION

Welcome to the *Six-Minute Thinking Skills* series. These workbooks are designed for busy parents and professionals who need easy-to-use and effective materials for working with learners who struggle with the thinking skills required for school success.

This workbook, *Visualization Skills,* provides step-by-step activities to quickly build the ability to visualize information while reading.

Visualizing is our ability to create mental pictures in our heads based on the text we read or the words we hear. It is one of the key skills required for reading comprehension.

Students who visualize as they read not only have a richer reading experience but can recall what they have read for longer periods of time.

Moreover, having a strong mental image of a text allows students to more accurately and effectively answer Higher

Order Thinking (HOT) questions, such as inferencing, prediction, etc.

If your learner struggles with reading comprehension, working on visualization skills should be high on your list of priorities.

ABOUT THIS WORKBOOK

Key details of this workbook are:

- Suitable for 1-1 or classroom use

  This book can be used in a classroom or with a single learner.

- Gradually increments difficulty

  Learners begin with simple visualization tasks, which gradually increment as the book progresses. By the end, learners visualize multi-paragraph fiction and non-fiction passages.

- No-prep. No extra materials required

  Everything needed is included in the book - except for a pencil or pen! The student can write their answers in the book, or use a piece of paper if the book needs to be reused. A few of the tasks require color pencils or crayons. These can be skipped if needed.

- Small chunks. Use any time

Our worksheets are designed for 'six-minute sessions.' Anytime you have a spare moment, your learner can accomplish the next incremental step in their learning journey.

The ability to visualize as you read is key for school and learning success. Support your struggling readers with this fun, engaging workbook that will build your learner's ability and confidence in this important skill.

HOW TO COACH A SIX-MINUTE SESSION

No student wants to spend extra time learning. Follow the guidelines in this section to promote efficient and motivating progress for your student.

1. Have a consistent and regular schedule.

Consistency and regularity are important if you want to reach a goal. So, choose a regular schedule for your six-minute sessions, get your learner's agreement and stick to it!

In a school setting, make this task a regular part of your students' day. In a home setting, aim for 3-4 times per week.

2. Devise a reward system.

Working on skill deficits is hard work for any learner. Appreciate your student's effort by building in a reward system.

This may include a reward when a specific number of exercises are finished, when tasks are completed correctly on the first try, or whatever specific goal will encourage your learner at this point in their journey.

Remember to reward based on effort as well as correctness.

3. Include time for review and correction.

After your student has completed the activity, review your student's work.

When identifying an error, make a positive statement and then provide the least information needed for the learner to make a correction. For example, prefer

> *Nice job. I can see you have drawn the desk and the pen. There is one more thing mentioned in the text. Can you see it and draw it?*

to

> *You forgot to draw the chair.*

The first method develops the student's ability to review their work and find the error. This valuable skill will lead to fewer errors in future worksheets.

The second method simply tells the student what to do.

Another good technique for reviewing is to ask your learner open questions. (Not Yes/No questions). If you see your learner create an image that does not fit the text, help them question their images. Ask questions like, "What does the text say about what the boy was doing?", "What did the text say about WHERE this was happening?"

Make sure that your learner always has a chance to physically correct their work.

4. Don't evaluate drawing skills

During the workbook, your learner sketches what he or she has pictured for a text. This drawing is a representation of the mental image that your learner has created.

The quality of the drawing is completely irrelevant. A simple sketch is all that is needed. The only requirement is that you can recognize — or your learner can explain — how the drawing matches the text.

Don't let your learner spend time elaborating the drawing or making it 'perfect'. A quick representation is all that is needed. It is the mental work to create the image that we want to build, not the manual proficiency to transfer it to the page.

For this reason we have quite small spaces available for the drawings in the workbook - to promote quick sketches instead of elaborate drawings. If your learner has fine motor issues and needs a bigger space, just grab some paper instead.

5. Do the whole book twice!

The first time you go through the workbook, follow the directions as written. This will help your learner build basic visualization skills.

When you reach the end, start back at the beginning, this time completing the exercises orally. This extra practice will develop your learner's visualization skills even further.

The second time through, instead of drawing their mental image, your learner will describe the images they are creating.

This is harder work for your learner, but is excellent practice for building visualization skills.

Make sure to use questioning to elicit further details from your learner.

6. Ask questions to get more details

A really important part of helping your learner develop visualization skills is to ask questions to help your learner develop a richer picture.

Use the nine visualization words below (taught in the workbook) to ask your learner for more details about their mental image.

WHAT, WHERE, WHEN, ACTION, EMOTION, RELATION, HOW, VISUAL DETAILS, OTHER SENSORY DETAILS

For example:

- Where is your picture happening?
- I can see you've drawn a house. What is it made of?
- Are there any smells?
- Is the train in front of the tree?

Two types of questions are recommended:

1. Open questions that use a WH word. These are words like WHO, WHAT, WHERE, etc. Answers to these questions are more detailed than answers to simple Yes/No questions.

2. Alternative options questions. These questions are best for learners who struggle with expressive language, or who are still getting used to describing their images. These are questions like:

- Is the train big or small?
- I am trying to picture the house you mentioned, is it one level or two?

Be careful of getting too detailed with your questions. Ask about the most important elements and don't spend time questioning for the exact size and color of a tiny flower in the background!

Think of your job as questioning for the types of elements that might be included in a summary.

To help you formulate your questions, samples for each question word can be found in the next chapter.

7. Most importantly....

Most importantly, make this a FUN experience with your learner!

Learning happens best when our brains are relaxed, not stressed. It is your job to make sure your student's brain stays ready to learn while doing this workbook. Build success upon success and celebrate every small achievement.

COACHING QUESTIONS

Use the question words and these sample questions as a starting point for your own questions.

WHAT

What things are in your picture?

What's the most noticeable part of your picture?

WHERE

Where is the boy in your picture?

What is around the boy in your picture?

WHEN

When is your picture happening?

Is it day or night time in your picture? How can you tell?

ACTION

What actions are people doing in your picture?

What movement is happening in your picture?

EMOTION

How are people feeling in your picture?

What are people's faces showing in your picture?

RELATION

What's at the front of your picture?

The train you mentioned, is that in front of the tree or behind the tree?

HOW

You said your boy was sitting. Is he sitting up straight or slouching down?

You mentioned a stream. How is the water flowing? Is it fast and deep, or shallow and slow?

VISUAL DETAILS

Tell me what the girl looks like. How old is she? What is she wearing?

How big is that tree?

OTHER SENSORY DETAILS

Are there any smells in your picture?

What sounds can the people in your picture hear?

VISUALIZATION EXERCISES

1. SINGLE WORD

Draw a picture of what you imagine for each word.

Cat

Castle

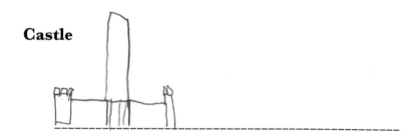

Dump Truck

Coaching Note: Encourage your learner to explain their drawing.

2. SINGLE WORD

Draw a picture of what you imagine for each word.

Computer

Mountain

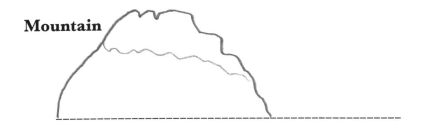

Artist

Coaching Note: Encourage your learner to explain their drawing.

3. ABSTRACT WORD

Draw a picture of what you imagine for each word.

Happy

Difficult

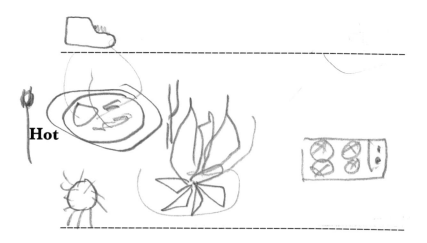

Coaching Note: Encourage your learner to explain their drawing.

4. ABSTRACT WORD

Draw a picture of what you imagine for each word.

Smooth

Medical

Slow

Coaching Note: Encourage your learner to explain their drawing.

5. PHRASE

Draw a picture of what you imagine for each description.

Wet dog

Broken cup

Happy girl

Coaching Note: Encourage your learner to explain their drawing.

6. PHRASE

Draw a picture of what you imagine for each description.

Sleepy boy

Dirty plate

Slow river

Coaching Note: Encourage your learner to explain their drawing.

7. PHRASE

Draw a picture of what you imagine for each description.

Large spotted frog

Tallest building

Full bus

Coaching Note: Encourage your learner to explain their drawing.

8. PHRASE

Draw a picture of what you imagine for each description.

Scary book

Weird picture

Dying tree

Coaching Note: Encourage your learner to explain their drawing.

9. PHRASE

Draw a picture of what you imagine for each description.

Wide awake

Super comfortable

Rock hard

Coaching Note: Encourage your learner to explain their drawing.

10. PHRASE

Draw a picture of what you imagine for each description.

Sneak attack

Soft touch

Under cover

Coaching Note: Encourage your learner to explain their drawing.

11. IMAGE WORDS - WHAT

Circle the words that mention WHAT is talked about: These are the people or things in the sentence.

Draw each thing that you circle.

The boy pulled the train.

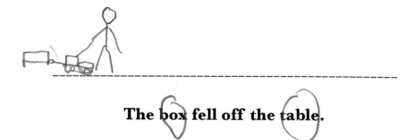

The box fell off the table.

Coaching Note: Make sure each object in the sentence is drawn.

12. IMAGE WORDS - WHAT

Circle the words that mention WHAT is talked about: These are the people or things in the sentence.

Draw each thing that you circle.

John opened the lid and looked inside the box. There was a tiny puppy looking back at him.

The highest building in the world is the Burj Khalifa. It is in Dubai.

13. IMAGE WORDS - WHERE

Underline the words that mention WHERE something is located.

Draw each location that you underline.

Katy stood at the entrance to the tunnel.

The rainforests of Brazil contain many animals.

Coaching Note: The key element is for learners to draw the location. If they draw other details from the text, that is okay, too.

14. IMAGE WORDS - WHERE

Underline the words that mention WHERE something is located.

Draw each location that you underline.

Tirak cleaned up the kitchen before turning on the television in the living room.

Liam kicked the ball hard, but instead of going into the goal, it went up into the air.

Coaching Note: The key element is for learners to draw the location. If they draw other details from the text, that is okay, too.

15. IMAGE WORDS - WHAT + WHERE

Underline the words that mention WHERE.

Circle the words that mention WHAT is talked about.

For each text, draw a picture that includes at least one WHAT item and one WHERE location.

Lisa loves inventing things. She has a special desk in the basement where she works on projects.

Australia has many amazing birds. Two famous ones are the kookaburra and the cockatoo.

----

16. IMAGE WORDS - WHEN

Circle the words that mention WHEN something happens.

Think about how this WHEN information changes or adds information to your picture.

Pluto was discovered in 1930.

_____

Kasen wants to be a superhero for Halloween.

_____

Yesterday the teacher told us that the assignment was due on Friday.

_____

We get pizza every Monday.

_____

I am always tired after soccer training.

_____

Coaching Note: Some examples contain more than one WHEN.

17. IMAGE WORDS - WHEN

Draw a picture that shows WHEN the events in the sentence happened.

It rained last night.

Kathy got dressed before breakfast.

----

18. IMAGE WORDS - WHEN + WHERE

Circle the words that mention WHERE something is located.

Underline the words that mention WHEN the events in the sentence happened.

Draw a picture that shows WHEN and WHERE.

The supermarket was quite busy early this morning.

The largest planet in the solar system is Jupiter. I saw it through a telescope at the science center last night.

----

19. IMAGE WORDS - ACTION

Circle the words that mention an ACTION that someone or something is doing.

Draw each action that you circle.

James ran for the bus.

Mariah drew a picture of a dog.

----

20. IMAGE WORDS - ACTION

Circle the words that mention an ACTION that someone or something is doing.

Draw each action that you circle.

The car whizzed by, splashing water on Jenna.

Shelley slammed the book on the desk.

----

21. IMAGE WORDS - WHAT + ACTION

Circle the words that mention WHAT people or items are mentioned in the sentence.

Underline the words that mention what ACTION is happening.

For each sentence, draw a picture that includes a WHAT and an ACTION.

The cat purred in Misha's lap.

You shouldn't give out personal information to people you don't know.

----

22. IMAGE WORDS - EMOTION

Circle the words that mention how someone is feeling.

Draw a picture that shows the feeling.

Kaisha excitedly opened the present.

The tiny puppy gave a mournful howl when the door closed.

Coaching Note: Make sure all parts of the drawing match the sentence.

23. IMAGE WORDS - EMOTION

Sometimes the emotions in a sentence aren't directly mentioned. But you can figure out the emotions from the other words in the sentence.

Glenn glared at the pile of homework.

How is Glenn feeling?

_____

Which word gave you the clue he was feeling that way?

_____

Reilly wiped the tears from her eyes.

How is Reilly feeling?

_____

Which words gave you the clue she was feeling that way?

_____

24. IMAGE WORDS - EMOTION

Sometimes the emotions in a sentence aren't directly mentioned. But you can figure out the emotions from the other words in the sentence.

Underline the words that convey emotions.

Dad shook his head as he reviewed Hayden's report card.

Tim pumped his fist in the air when he heard his favorite team won.

I asked my friend Kelly if she passed the exam. She just bit her lip and looked away.

Jemma got home 20 minutes late. Her mom was standing by the door with her arms crossed.

The kindergarten class streamed out of the school, yelling and screaming as they scampered towards the playground.

The kindergarten class streamed out of the school, yelling and screaming as they raced away from the smoky building.

Coaching Note: Make sure to discuss the last two examples as they are a little trickier.

25. IMAGE WORDS - EMOTION + ACTION

Circle the words that convey EMOTIONS.

Underline the words that mention ACTIONS.

For each text, draw a picture that shows the EMOTION and an ACTION.

After hearing a strange sound outside, Lina nervously peered through the window.

Mom opened the box and screamed.

Coaching Note: For the second example, ask your learner to consider alternate interpretations.

26. IMAGE WORDS - RELATION

Some words tell us how items or events are situated in RELATION to each other. One thing might be ABOVE another. One event might happen BEFORE another.

Underline any words that describe a RELATION.

Draw a picture to match the sentence.

The kitten hid under the chair.

The sun lifted above the trees.

----

27. IMAGE WORDS - RELATION

Underline any words that describe a RELATION.

Yesterday we had spaghetti for dinner. Today we have pizza.

Draw the meal that was eaten second.

Before Caleb could blow out the candles, the cake exploded.

Draw what happened first.

----

28. IMAGE WORDS - RELATION + ACTION

Circle the words that identify an ACTION.

Underline the words that describe a RELATION.

Draw a picture to match the sentence.

The cheetah snuck up behind its prey and pounced.

Greg grabbed the dishes from the table and put them in the dishwasher.

----

29. IMAGE WORDS - HOW

Some words tell us HOW things happen - fast, slow, sadly, etc.

Underline any words that describe HOW.

Draw a picture to match the sentence.

Pia slowly patted the cat to help it calm down.

Carmen quickly ran out of the rain.

----

30. IMAGE WORDS - HOW

Underline any words that describe HOW.

Draw a picture to match the text.

Gina dashed for the bus.

Henry yelled, "Stop!"

Coaching Note: Some words contain an ACTION and a HOW. For example, 'dash' conveys that Gina ran and also that she ran quickly.

31. IMAGE WORDS - HOW

Underline any words that describe HOW.

Draw a picture to match the text.

Kelsie slammed the door with a bang.

Dylan crept into the dark cave, listening carefully for any sound.

----

32. IMAGE WORDS - HOW + RELATION

Circle the words that identify HOW.

Underline the words that describe a RELATION.

Draw a picture to match the sentence.

Callie gently put the delicate vase on the table.

The soccer ball slammed into the window, creating a large crack from top to bottom.

----

33. IMAGE WORDS - VISUAL DETAILS

Some words tell us what things look like. These are VISUAL DETAILS.

Underline any words that describe a VISUAL DETAIL.

Draw a picture to match the sentence.

Nyah wore her long, striped dress and sparkly shoes.

Coaching Note: Any word that helps you refine the appearance of something can be a visual detail. For example, 'young' in 'young horse' helps you picture a smaller horse that is probably full of energy.

34. IMAGE WORDS - VISUAL DETAILS

Underline any words that describe a VISUAL DETAIL.

Draw a picture to match the text.

Hallie wears a blue rain jacket when she plays soccer in the pouring rain.

Phillip loves to climb tall trees and dig deep holes in the garden. He pretends he is a scary pirate searching for treasure.

----

35. IMAGE WORDS - VISUAL DETAILS

Underline any words that describe a VISUAL DETAIL.

Draw a picture to match the text.

The leaves in the garden were starting to turn yellow.

The roof was so steep that snow slid right off it.

Coaching Note: In the first example, help your learner infer that most of the leaves on the tree are still green.

36. IMAGE WORDS - VISUAL DETAIL + RELATION

Circle any words that identify a VISUAL DETAIL.

Underline any words that describe a RELATION.

Draw a picture to match the sentence.

The small black box was hidden behind the broken chair.

The fluffy snowflakes tumbled silently from the grey sky.

----

37. IMAGE WORDS - OTHER SENSORY DETAILS

Good writers use all five senses to convey information. Look in the following sentences for OTHER SENSORY DETAILS such as taste, touch, sound and smell.

Underline any words that describe an OTHER SENSORY DETAIL.

Draw a picture to match the text.

The sharp wire caught on Sasha's sweater. She groaned when she saw the long rip in the soft fabric.

Chris bit into the dry cookie. It tasted of... chile pepper! His mouth was on fire!

Coaching Note: 'Groan' conveys a sound as well as an emotion.

38. IMAGE WORDS - OTHER SENSORY DETAILS

Underline any words that describe an OTHER SENSORY DETAIL.

Draw a picture to match the text.

Pierre felt the rumble of the approaching train. He clapped his hands over his ears just as the shrill whistle sounded.

Brakes screeched. Horns blew. Then came the sound of crunching metal.

Coaching Note: Help your learner infer the visuals of the last example.

39. IMAGE WORDS - OTHER SENSORY DETAIL + ACTION

Circle any words that identify an ACTION.

Underline any words that describe a SENSORY DETAIL.

Draw a picture to match the text.

The snow crunched under Alan's feet as he trudged to school.

Jacob heard the hiss of escaping air. Oh, no. His tire was flat.

----

40. VISUAL RECALL: PART 1

Look at the picture below for up to 30 seconds. Try to visualize the picture in your mind.

'Visualize' means using your imagination to make the picture in your mind. For some people, closing their eyes makes it easier to visualize.

When you can visualize the picture, turn the page and follow the instructions.

VISUAL RECALL: PART 2

Visualize the picture from the previous page in your head. Note down all the details you can remember in the table. No going back to check!

Some details may not be shown in the picture.

WHAT	
WHERE	
WHEN	
ACTION	
EMOTION	
RELATION	
SENSORY DETAILS (see, touch, taste, sound, smell)	

How many details did you visualize? _____

Write a one sentence summary of the picture.

_____

41. VISUAL RECALL: PART 1

Look at the picture below for up to 30 seconds. Try to visualize the picture in your mind.

'Visualize' means using your imagination to make the picture in your mind. For some people, closing their eyes makes it easier to visualize.

When you can visualize the picture, turn the page and follow the instructions.

43. VISUAL RECALL: PART 2

Visualize the picture from the previous page in your head. Note down all the details you can remember in the table. No going back to check!

Some details may not be shown in the picture.

WHAT	
WHERE	
WHEN	
ACTION	
EMOTION	
RELATION	
SENSORY DETAILS (see, touch, taste, sound, smell)	

How many details did you visualize? _____

Write a one sentence summary of the picture.

_____

42. VISUAL RECALL: PART 1

Look at the picture below for up to 30 seconds. Try to visualize the picture in your mind.

'Visualize' means using your imagination to make the picture in your mind. For some people, closing their eyes makes it easier to visualize.

When you can visualize the picture, turn the page and follow the instructions.

43. VISUAL RECALL: PART 2

Visualize the picture from the previous page in your head. Note down all the details you can remember in the table. No going back to check!

Some details may not be shown in the picture.

WHAT	
WHERE	
WHEN	
ACTION	
EMOTION	
RELATION	
SENSORY DETAILS (see, touch, taste, sound, smell)	

How many details did you visualize? _____

Write a one sentence summary of the picture.

----

43. SPATIAL MANIPULATION

Look at the picture below.

Visualize this image in your mind and now flip it upside down.

Draw the new picture in the space below.

44. SPATIAL MANIPULATION

Look at the picture below.

In your mind, turn it 90 degrees to the right (one quarter turn.)

Now replace the three small circles with triangles.

Draw the new picture in the space below.

45. SPATIAL MANIPULATION

Look at the picture below.

In your mind, switch the left and right small hearts.

Put the large heart to the right of the three small hearts.

Put a new small grey heart below the large heart.

Draw the new picture in the space below.

46. LETTER SEQUENCE

Look at the letter sequence below and visualize it in your mind.

Cover up the letters and answer the questions. Don't peek!

B C F D

1. What is the second letter?
2. What is the last letter?
3. List the letters in reverse order.

Answer the same questions for the following sequence.

Don't peek!

H N A E G

47. LETTER SEQUENCE

Look at the letter sequence below and visualize it in your mind.

Cover up the letters and answer the questions. Don't peek!

LKWRA

1. What letter is to the left of K?
2. What letter is in second last position?
3. What is the middle letter?

Answer the same questions for the following sequence.

Don't peek!

BRDKY

48. LETTER SEQUENCE

Look at the letter sequence below and visualize it in your mind.

Cover up the letters and answer the questions. Don't peek!

FDHETP

1. What are the third and fourth letters?
2. What letter is before H?
3. Which of the letters comes earliest in the alphabet?

Answer the same questions for the following sequence.

Don't peek!

SXCIQHD

49. VISUAL DIRECTIONS - INSTRUCTIONS

Read the drawing directions below and visualize what you need to draw.

Reread the directions if you need to. When you have a good picture in your mind of what you need to draw, turn the page and draw the picture.

Once you have turned the page, don't look back. Just do your best.

DRAWING INSTRUCTIONS

1. Draw a large circle.
2. In the middle of the circle, draw two small circles next to each other.
3. Color the small circles black.
4. Draw a smiling mouth in the bottom half of the circle.

VISUAL DIRECTIONS - DRAWING

Keep the image in your mind and draw the picture below.

50. VISUAL DIRECTIONS - INSTRUCTIONS

Read the drawing directions below and visualize what you need to draw.

Reread the directions if you need to. When you have a good picture in your mind of what you need to draw, turn the page and draw the picture.

Once you have turned the page, don't look back. Just do your best.

DRAWING INSTRUCTIONS

1. Draw a small circle in the middle of the page.
2. At the top of the circle, draw a short line that goes straight up.
3. At the bottom of the circle, draw a short line that goes straight down.
4. On the right hand side of the circle, draw a short line that goes to the right.
5. On the left hand side of the circle, draw a short line that goes to the left.

VISUAL DIRECTIONS - DRAWING

Keep the image in your mind and draw the picture below.

51. VISUAL DIRECTIONS - INSTRUCTIONS

Read the drawing directions below and visualize what you need to draw.

Reread the directions if you need to. When you have a good picture in your mind of what you need to draw, turn the page and draw the picture.

Once you have turned the page, don't look back. Just do your best.

DRAWING INSTRUCTIONS

1. Draw a medium-sized square.
2. Draw a triangle sitting on top of the square. The base of the triangle should be the same size as the square.
3. Put your pencil at the bottom of the square in the middle.
4. Draw a line up, across and then down to make a rectangle inside the square.

VISUAL DIRECTIONS - DRAWING

Keep the image in your mind and draw the picture below.

52. ITEM MEMORY

Look at the pictures below and visualize them in your mind.

After 30 seconds, cover up the pictures and list everything that you can remember.

Don't peek!

----

53. ITEM MEMORY

Look at the pictures below and visualize them in your mind.

After 30 seconds, cover up the pictures and list everything that you can remember.

Don't peek!

----

54. ITEM MEMORY

Look at the pictures below and visualize them in your mind.

After 30 seconds, cover up the pictures and list everything that you can remember.

Don't peek!

_____

_____

_____

_____

_____

_____

55. ITEM MEMORY

Look at the pictures below and visualize them in your mind.

After 30 seconds, cover up the pictures and list everything that you can remember.

Don't peek!

----

56. MOTION FROM TEXT: INSTRUCTIONS

Read the text once or twice. Visualize the scene as you read, making sure to include the characters' movement in your 'brain movie.'

Cover the text. Now stand up and act out the story in the text. Include as many details as you can remember.

Turn the page and complete the tasks. Don't look back! (Only do one text at a time.)

TEXT 1

John waited at the bus stop. It was raining, so he kept his umbrella up. Soon the bus came. He closed his umbrella and climbed onto the bus. He got a seat in the front row.

Act out this story now.

TEXT 2

When Shelley was walking home from school, she heard a noise coming from the tall bushes next to the path. Curious, she stopped and pulled aside one of the branches. A tiny kitten sat shivering in a nest of leaves. She carefully picked it up and gave it a soft pat. The kitten purred.

Coaching Note: Use questioning to help your learner include as many details from the text as possible into their movements.

MOTION FROM TEXT: TEXT 1 PART 2

- On the left, draw what John was doing first.
- On the right, draw what John was doing last.

TEXT 2 PART 2

- On the left, draw what Shelley was doing first.
- On the right, draw what Shelley was doing last.

57. MOTION FROM TEXT: INSTRUCTIONS

Read the text once or twice. Visualize the scene as you read, making sure to include the characters' movement in your 'brain movie.'

Cover the text. Now stand up and act out the story in the text. Include as many details as you can remember.

Turn the page and complete the tasks. Don't look back! (Only do one text at a time.)

TEXT 3

"There's a dust storm coming," Mom shouted. "Help me shut the windows and doors."

Willa dashed to the living room and slammed the windows closed. Looking through the glass, she could see a thick wall of dust roaring towards the house.

Act out this story now.

TEXT 4

Shawn pushed open the gate and laughed as his dog Daisy bounded toward him with a loud bark.

"Hey, Daisy!" He patted Daisy's soft head with both hands. "Where's mom?"

Just as he said that, his mom opened the front door, holding a plate of delicious-smelling cookies.

MOTION FROM TEXT: TEXT 3 PART 2

- On the left, draw what Willa was doing first.
- On the right, draw what Willa was doing last.

TEXT 4 PART 2

- On the left, draw what Shawn was doing first.
- On the right, draw what Shawn was doing last.

58. TWO SENTENCES TO IMAGE: INSTRUCTIONS

Read the text below. Visualize the story as you read. Include as many details as you can.

Next, turn the page and draw an image from the movie you created in your brain. Include as many details as you can. Don't look back!

Do one text at a time.

TEXT 1

Lightning strikes the surface of the Earth about 100 times per second. Lightning storms are most common during spring and summer.

Turn the page now.

TEXT 2

The school was holding a knitting contest. Julia didn't know how to knit so she asked her grandma to teach her.

TWO SENTENCES TO IMAGE: PART 2

TEXT 1

Draw a picture from your brain movie.

TEXT 2

Draw a picture from your brain movie.

Coaching Note: Use questions to help learners create more detailed mental images/drawings.

59. TWO SENTENCES TO IMAGE: INSTRUCTIONS

Read the text below. Visualize the story as you read. Include as many details as you can.

Next, turn the page and draw an image from the movie you created in your brain. Include as many details as you can. Don't look back!

Do one text at a time.

TEXT 3

Antibiotics are drugs that kill infections. There are many different types of antibiotics.

Turn the page now.

TEXT 4

Captain James Cook landed in Australia in 1770. The ship he captained was called the Endeavour.

TEXT 3

Draw a picture from your brain movie.

TEXT 4

Draw a picture from your brain movie.

Coaching Note: Use questions to help learners create more detailed mental images/drawings.

60. TWO SENTENCES TO IMAGE: INSTRUCTIONS

Read the text below. Visualize the story as you read. Include as many details as you can.

Next, turn the page and draw an image from the movie you created in your brain. Include as many details as you can. Don't look back!

Do one text at a time.

TEXT 5

The school sports day is usually very loud and busy. Groups of students compete in fun sports and games.

Turn the page now.

TEXT 6

If I could have anything I wished for, I would wish for a pair of magic glasses. These glasses would let me see all sorts of extra information about anything I looked at.

TEXT 5

Draw a picture from your brain movie.

TEXT 6

Draw a picture from your brain movie.

Coaching Note: Use questions to help your learner create more detailed mental images/drawings.

61. TWO SENTENCES TO TABLE: PART 1

Read the text below. Visualize the story as you read. Include as many details as you can in your brain movie.

Next, turn the page and list all the details you remember from your brain movie. Don't look back!

Tigers live in Asia, but may soon go extinct. In 2010, there were only 3,100 tigers left in the wild.

Coaching Note: Explain any words that your learner does not understand. You can't make an image if you don't know what to visualize!

TWO SENTENCES TO TABLE: PART 2

Note down all the details you can remember from your brain movie or from the story in the table below. No going back to check!

Some sections of the table may not have any details.

WHAT	
WHERE	
WHEN	
ACTION	
EMOTION	
RELATION	
SENSORY DETAILS (see, touch, taste, sound, smell)	

How many details did you remember?_____

Write a one sentence summary of the story.

_____

_____

62. TWO SENTENCES TO TABLE: PART 1

Read the text below. Visualize the story as you read. Include as many details as you can in your brain movie.

Next, turn the page and list all the details you remember from your brain movie. Don't look back!

Gold panning is a fun activity and you might end up finding some gold! To pan for gold, you need a shallow dish and a creek where you can scoop sand and water.

Coaching Note: Explain any words that your learner does not understand. You can't make an image if you don't know what to visualize!

TWO SENTENCES TO TABLE: PART 2

Note down all the details you can remember from your brain movie or from the story in the table below. No going back to check!

Some sections of the table may not have any details.

WHAT	
WHERE	
WHEN	
ACTION	
EMOTION	
RELATION	
SENSORY DETAILS (see, touch, taste, sound, smell)	

How many details did you remember?_____

Write a one sentence summary of the story.

_____

_____

63. TWO SENTENCES TO TABLE: PART 1

Read the text below. Visualize the story as you read. Include as many details as you can in your brain movie.

Next, turn the page and list all the details you remember from your brain movie. Don't look back!

Today was the first day that Carrie was allowed to walk to school by herself. She waved goodbye to her mom and started up the street, excited and nervous.

TWO SENTENCES TO TABLE: PART 2

Note down all the details you can remember from your brain movie or from the story in the table below. No going back to check!

Some sections of the table may not have any details.

WHAT	
WHERE	
WHEN	
ACTION	
EMOTION	
RELATION	
SENSORY DETAILS (see, touch, taste, sound, smell)	

How many details did you remember?_____

Write a one sentence summary of the story.

_____

_____

64. TWO SENTENCES TO QUESTIONS: PART 1

Read the text below. Visualize the story as you read. Include as many details as you can.

Next, turn the page and answer the questions about the brain movie you created. Don't look back!

Celia walked home from school and then dumped her backpack in the kitchen. She was super thirsty, so she grabbed the jug of cool water from the fridge.

TWO SENTENCES TO QUESTIONS: PART 2

Visualize the story from the previous page in your head and answer these questions.

How old did you picture Celia?

What was she wearing?

What did you picture for her backpack? Give two details.

What room was Celia in when she arrived home?

What actions did Celia do when she got home?

----

65. TWO SENTENCES TO QUESTIONS: PART 1

Read the text below. Visualize the story as you read. Include as many details as you can.

Next, turn the page and answer the questions about the brain movie you created. Don't look back!

Sarah wanted to learn how to use a map and compass. She called up her Uncle Mark and asked him if he could teach her.

TWO SENTENCES TO QUESTIONS: PART 2

Visualize the story from the previous page in your head and answer these questions.

Who wanted to learn about using a map and compass?

Who already knows how to use a map and compass?

What do you picture for the word 'compass'?

How did Sarah find a teacher to teach her how to use a map and compass?

In your picture, where was Sarah when she called her uncle?

----

66. TWO SENTENCES TO QUESTIONS: PART 1

Read the text below. Visualize the story as you read. Include as many details as you can.

Next, turn the page and answer the questions about the brain movie you created. Don't look back!

Jason's favorite activity is riding roller coasters. He has been on fifteen different roller coasters in his life.

TWO SENTENCES TO QUESTIONS: PART 2

Visualize the story from the previous page in your head and answer these questions.

Describe 3 different things that are in the movie you visualized.

What emotions and actions are in your movie?

What does Jason look like in your movie?

----

67. PARAGRAPH TO IMAGE: INSTRUCTIONS

Read the text below. Visualize the story as you read. Include as many details as you can.

Next, turn the page and draw a picture from your brain movie. Include as many details as you can. Don't look back!

TEXT 1

Climates vary from place to place. Near the equator, the weather is always warm and days are about the same length year round. Near the north and south poles, the weather gets extremely cold and in summer, the days are very long.

Turn the page now.

TEXT 2

It was Kelly's first day at a new school and she was nervous. Her mom took her to the school office and Kelly met a girl named Lana who would be her buddy. Lana took Kelly to her new class and made Kelly feel much more comfortable.

PARAGRAPH TO IMAGE: PART 2

TEXT 1

Draw a picture from your brain movie.

TEXT 2

Draw a picture from your brain movie.

Coaching Note: Use questions to elicit more details about your learner's images.

68. PARAGRAPH TO IMAGE: INSTRUCTIONS

Read the text below. Visualize the story as you read. Include as many details as you can.

Next, turn the page and draw a picture from your brain movie. Include as many details as you can. Don't look back!

TEXT 3

Penguins are a type of bird. They live in the water and on land. Wild penguins live in the southern hemisphere only. They mostly eat fish and squid.

Turn the page now.

TEXT 4

Henry went to stay at a fancy hotel with his grandma. After they checked in, they wheeled their bags up to the room. The room had a big balcony, two huge beds and a jacuzzi in the bathroom. A little button next to the tub turned on the bubbles.

PARAGRAPH TO IMAGE: PART 2

TEXT 3

Draw a picture from your brain movie.

TEXT 4

Draw a picture from your brain movie.

Coaching Note: Use questions to elicit more details about your learner's images.

69. PARAGRAPH TO IMAGE: INSTRUCTIONS

Read the text below. Visualize the story as you read. Include as many details as you can.

Next, turn the page and draw a picture from your brain movie. Include as many details as you can. Don't look back!

TEXT 5

Last Sunday, John and his father went to the zoo. John had never been before. He was very excited.

The first animal they saw was a lion. After that they saw monkeys and elephants. The best part of the day was when John got to feed the colorful parrots.

Turn the page now.

TEXT 6

The fastest train in the world is in the city of Shanghai in China. The train is called the Shanghai Maglev.

Magnets lift the train off the track so it can go really fast. On normal days, the top speed of the train is 268 miles per hour. It can carry 574 people.

TEXT 5

Draw a picture from your brain movie.

TEXT 6

Draw a picture from your brain movie.

Coaching Note: Use questions to elicit more details about your learner's images.

Read the text below. Visualize the story as you read. Include as many details as you can in your brain movie.

Next, turn the page and list all the details you remember from your brain movie. Don't look back!

Gold panning is a fun activity and you might end up finding some gold! To pan for gold, you need a shallow dish and a creek where you can scoop sand and water.

Swirl the sand and water around your pan and gradually let it spill out over the edge. The heavier gold will be left at the bottom of your pan.

Coaching Note: This text intentionally builds on the previous gold panning text.

PARAGRAPH TO TABLE: PART 2

Note down all the details you can remember from your brain movie or from the story in the table below. No going back to check!

Some sections of the table may not have any details.

WHAT	
WHERE	
WHEN	
ACTION	
EMOTION	
RELATION	
SENSORY DETAILS (see, touch, taste, sound, smell)	

How many details did you remember?_____

Write a one sentence summary of the story.

_____

_____

71. PARAGRAPH TO TABLE: PART 1

Read the text below. Visualize the story as you read. Include as many details as you can in your brain movie.

Next, turn the page and list all the details you remember from your brain movie. Don't look back!

A volcano is a mountain where lava erupts from the top of the mountain.

Lava is rock that is so hot that it has become a liquid. Lava can burst from the top of a volcano or flow down its sides like a river.

Volcanoes can be found all over the earth, but most are found around the edge of the Pacific Ocean. This is called the Ring of Fire.

PARAGRAPH TO TABLE: PART 2

Note down all the details you can remember from your brain movie or from the story in the table below. No going back to check!

Some sections of the table may not have any details.

WHAT	
WHERE	
WHEN	
ACTION	
EMOTION	
RELATION	
SENSORY DETAILS (see, touch, taste, sound, smell)	

How many details did you remember?_____

Write a one or two sentence summary of the story.

_____

_____

72. PARAGRAPH TO TABLE: PART 1

Read the text below. Visualize the story as you read. Include as many details as you can in your brain movie.

Next, turn the page and list all the details you remember from your brain movie. Don't look back!

Today Patty went on a plane for the first time. Before she left home, her stomach felt a little yucky, but she was also excited.

At the airport she forgot her nerves because there was so much going on. First she checked in, then she waited at the gate. Soon after that she got on the plane and was ready to take off!

PARAGRAPH TO TABLE: PART 2

Note down all the details you can remember from your brain movie or from the story in the table below. No going back to check!

Some sections of the table may not have any details.

WHAT	
WHERE	
WHEN	
ACTION	
EMOTION	
RELATION	
SENSORY DETAILS (see, touch, taste, sound, smell)	

How many details did you remember?_____

Write a one or two sentence summary of the story.

_____

_____

73. PARAGRAPH TO QUESTIONS: PART 1

Read the text below. Visualize the story as you read. Include as many details as you can.

Next, turn the page and answer the questions about the brain movie you created. Don't look back!

Did you know that some plants eat animals?

The Venus flytrap feeds on small animals like ants, flies and moths. The Venus flytrap has leaves shaped like a clam. When an animal lands on the leaves, the leaves snap shut.

The plant then lets out a liquid that helps digest the animal.

PARAGRAPH TO QUESTIONS: PART 2

Visualize the story from the previous page in your head and answer these questions.

What color are the leaves of your Venus flytrap?

In your movie, where is your Venus flytrap?

How does the Venus flytrap catch a fly?

How big is your Venus flytrap?

What other details can you see in your movie?

Coaching Note: Use questions to elicit more details about your learner's image.

74. PARAGRAPH TO QUESTIONS: PART 1

Read the text below. Visualize the story as you read. Include as many details as you can.

Next, turn the page and answer the questions about the brain movie you created. Don't look back!

There are two different types of camels. Arabian camels have one hump. Camels from Asia have two humps.

Many people think the humps are to hold water. This is not true. The humps have fat inside. The fat keeps their body cool. Camels need this because they live in hot deserts.

PARAGRAPH TO QUESTIONS: PART 2

Visualize the story from the previous page in your head and answer these questions.

Describe the camels in your brain movie. How are they the same and how are they different?

_____

_____

_____

Where are the camels in your movie?

_____

_____

What information about a camel's hump do you remember?

_____

_____

75. PARAGRAPH TO QUESTIONS: PART 1

Read the text below. Visualize the story as you read. Include as many details as you can.

Next, turn the page and answer the questions about the brain movie you created. Don't look back!

Last summer, Trenna's family went to Ape cave in Washington State. Ape Cave is a lava tube. It is shaped like a tube and was made from flowing lava.

Trenna's whole family went into the cave, even her 2-year-old brother. When they turned off their flashlights, it was completely black. Trenna couldn't see a thing. She was a little scared.

PARAGRAPH QUESTIONS: PART 2

Visualize the story from the previous page in your head and answer these questions.

Describe what Trenna looks like in your movie.

_____

_____

_____

How many people are in Trenna's family in your movie?

_____

_____

Where is Trenna in your movie? What is around her?

_____

_____

WHAT NEXT?

If this is your first time completing the workbook, your next step should be to complete the workbook again, this time doing it orally.

Check out the coaching instructions at the beginning of the book for more information on the oral approach.

By the time you have completed the oral version of the workbook, your learner will be able to describe the images they are making as they read short paragraphs.

Your next step is to transfer this skill to reading real books.

Choose easy, visual stories and build up your learner's stamina at visualizing while they read. Start with questioning their mental image every few sentences and build up to a page or more at a time.

If you feel like your learner needs a little more practice, we also have a 'More Visualization Skills' book which builds on the current 'Visualization Skills' workbook to provide additional, scaffolded practice for learners building their comprehension skills.

The first quarter of 'More Visualization Skills' mimics the step-by-step activities found in the original workbook, building visualization skills from single words to 2-sentence paragraphs. The remainder of the book builds skill from 2-sentence paragraphs to short multi-paragraph texts. This positions your learner for a successful transition to real books.

BEFORE YOU GO

If you found this book useful, please leave a short review on your favorite online bookstore. It makes an amazing difference for independent publishers like Happy Frog Press. Just two sentences will do!

ADDITIONAL RESOURCES

We also have other books to support your learner.

Don't forget to look for other workbooks in the **Six-Minute Thinking Skills** series.

Your learners might also benefit from our **Six-Minute Social Skills series**.

The workbooks in this series build core social skills for kids who have social skills challenges, such as those with Autism, Asperger's and ADHD.

Although numbered, these books can be used in any order.

CERTIFICATE
OF
ACHIEVEMENT

THIS CERTIFICATE IS AWARDED TO

_____

IN RECOGNITION OF

_____

_____   _____
DATE   SIGNATURE

101

Made in the USA
Las Vegas, NV
18 August 2021

28368702R10068